THE BEAUTY OF AMERICA
IN GREAT AMERICAN ART

By the Editors of COUNTRY BEAUTIFUL

Editorial Direction: Michael P. Dineen
Edited by Robert L. Polley
Art Direction and Design by Robert W. Pradt

THE BEAUTY
In Great

Preface by Eric F. Goldman

Introduction by Tracy Atkinson
Director, Milwaukee Art Center

OF AMERICA
American Art

With selections from the writings
of renowned American authors

Published by Country Beautiful Foundation, Inc., Waukesha, Wisconsin

COUNTRY BEAUTIFUL: Michael P. Dineen, *Publisher and Editorial Director;* Robert L. Polley, *Executive Editor;* Robert W. Pradt, *Art Director;* Charles R. Fowler, *Managing Editor;* Kenneth L. Schmitz, James H. Robb, *Senior Editors;* Robert Fehring, *Art Assistant;* Sharon G. Armao, Vicki Russi, *Assistants.*

The Editors are grateful to the following publishers, authors and other copyright holders for permission to include the following copyright material in this volume: Appleton-Century, Book Publishers, for excerpt from "The Cod-Fisher" by Joseph C. Lincoln. The Bobbs-Merrill Company, Inc. for excerpt from *Collected Poems,* copyright 1931, R. 1959 by Richard Burton, reprinted by permission of the publishers, The Bobbs-Merrill Company, Inc. The Christian Science Monitor for excerpt from "Sea Town" by Frances Frost. Hubert T. Delany for excerpt from "The Mask," by Clarissa Scott Delany. Diablo Press for excerpt by Herb Caen from *Our San Francisco* © 1964 by Diablo Press. Dodd, Mead & Company for excerpt from "Twilight" from *Curtains* by Hazel Hall, copyright, 1921 by Dodd, Mead & Company. Alice Henson Ernst for excerpt from "Ya-Ihl's Song to the North Wind." Edna Ferber and her co-partners for excerpt from *Cimarron,* Copyright 1929, 1930 by Edna Ferber. Marguerite F. Fetcher for excerpt from "Spring is like a perhaps hand." Copyright, 1925, by E. E. Cummings. Reprinted from his volume *Poems 1923-1954* by permission of Harcourt, Brace & World, Inc., for excerpt from "Ripe Corn" from *Good Morning, America,* copyright, 1928, 1956, by Carl Sandburg. Reprinted by permission of Harcourt, Brace & World, Inc. Harcourt, Brace & World, Inc., for excerpt from "Two Funerals" from *Selected Poems and Parodies* by Louis Untermeyer, copyright, 1914, by Harcourt, Brace & World, Inc.; copyright, 1942 by Louis Untermeyer. Reprinted by permission of Harcourt, Brace & World, Inc. Harcourt, Brace & World, Inc., for excerpt from "Sun and Cloud" from *Bullet-Hunting and Other New Poems,* copyright, 1960, by Melville Cane. Reprinted by permission of Harcourt, Brace & World, Inc. Harcourt, Brace & World, Inc., for excerpt from "a wind has blown the rain away and blown." Copyright, 1923, 1951, by E. E. Cummings. Reprinted from his volume *Poems 1923-1954* by permission of Harcourt, Brace & World, Inc. Harcourt, Brace & World, Inc., for excerpt from "Improved Farm Land" from *Slabs of the Sunburnt West* by Carl Sandburg, copyright, 1922, by Harcourt, Brace & World, Inc.; copyright, 1950, by Carl Sandburg. Reprinted by permission of Harcourt, Brace & World, Inc. Harper & Row, Publishers, for excerpt from "The City" in *Poems of Five Decades* by Max Eastman. Copyright 1942, 1954 by Max Eastman. Reprinted by permission of Harper & Row, Publishers. Hastings House, Publishers, Inc., for excerpt from *The Buffalo Hunters* by Mari Sandoz, copyright, 1954 by Mari Sandoz. Hill & Wang, Inc., Publishers, for excerpt from "December Setting" from *Collected and New Poems 1924-1963* by Mark Van Doren. Copyright © 1963 by Mark Van Doren. Reprinted by permission of Hill & Wang, Inc. Holt, Rinehart and Winston, Inc. for excerpt from "Homestead" from *Collected Poems* by Horace Gregory. Copyright 1941 by Horace Gregory. Reprinted by permission of Holt, Rinehart and Winston, Inc. Houghton Mifflin Company for one excerpt each from "A Spring Day," "New York at Night," by Amy Lowell; also for excerpts from *In the Catskills* by John Burroughs; also for excerpt from *The Heart of John Burroughs Journals* edited by Clara Barrus; and also for excerpt from *Across the Wide Missouri* by Bernard De Voto. John Howell for excerpt from "Sails" by George Sterling. Alfred A. Knopf, Inc., for "Golden Bough." Copyright 1932 by Alfred A. Knopf, and renewed 1960 by Edwina C. Rubenstein. Reprinted from *Collected Poems of Elinor Wylie* by permission of the publisher. Alfred A. Knopf, Inc., for excerpt from "Persistent Explorer." Copyright 1927 by Alfred A. Knopf, Inc., and renewed 1955 by John Crowe Ransom. Reprinted from *Selected Poems,* Revised Edition, by John Crowe Ransom, by permission of the publisher. Alfred A. Knopf, Inc., for excerpt from Sonnet XXXII by Frederick Goddard Tuckerman. Copyright 1931 by Alfred A. Knopf, Inc. Reprinted from *The Sonnets of Frederick Goddard Tuckerman* by permission of the publisher. Liveright Publishing Corporation for excerpt from "The Bridge" from *The Collected*

Poems of Hart Crane. By Permission of LIVERIGHT, Publishers, N.Y. Copyright © R, 1961, by LIVERIGHT Publishing Corp. Liveright Publishing Corporation for excerpt from "The Cloud" from *A Treasury of Humorous Verse,* by Samuel Hoffenstein. By permission of LIVERIGHT, Publishers, N.Y. Copyright © R, 1956, by David Hoffenstein. Little, Brown and Company, Publishers for excerpt from "The bustle in a house," from *Poems by Emily Dickinson.* The Macmillan Company for excerpt from "Mainland-Woman's Return" from *Collected Poems* by Robert P. Tristram Coffin. Copyright 1942 by The Macmillan Co. Reprinted with permission of the Macmillan Co. The Macmillan Company for excerpt from "Winter Is My Year" from *Collected Poems* by Robert P. Tristram Coffin. Copyright 1945 by The Macmillan Co. Reprinted with permission of The Macmillan Co. The Macmillan Company for excerpt from "February" from *Rivers to the Sea* by Sara Teasdale. Copyright 1915 by The Macmillan Co. Renewed 1943 by Mamie T. Wheless. Reprinted with permission of The Macmillan Co. The Macmillan Company for excerpt from "Hillcrest" from *Man Against the Sky* by Edward Arlington Robinson. Copyright 1916 by The Macmillan Co., renewed 1944 by Ruth Nivison. Reprinted with permission of The Macmillan Co. Ann Leslie Moore for excerpt from "Streets in Dislocation, Stolid Snow . . ." by Merrill Moore. William Morrow and Company, Inc. for excerpt from *The Desert Year* by Joseph Wood Krutch. Copyright, 1951 and 1952, by Joseph Wood Krutch. Harold Ober Associates Incorporated for excerpt from "Jazztet Muted" from *Ask Your Mama: Twelve Moods for Jazz* by Langston Hughes. Copyright © 1959, 1961 by Langston Hughes. Reprinted by permission of Harold Ober Associates Incorporated. Oxford University Press, Inc. for excerpt from "Music I heard with you" from *Collected Poems* by Conrad Aiken. Copyright 1953 by Conrad Aiken. Reprinted by permission of Oxford University Press, Inc. Norman Holmes Pearson for excerpt from "The Helmsman" by H. D. Reprinted by permission of copyright owner, Norman Holmes Pearson. Putnam's & Coward-McCann for excerpt from *An Almanac for Moderns* by Donald Culross Peattie. Copyright, 1935, by Donald Culross Peattie. Random House, Inc. for excerpt from "The Old Man," by William Faulkner. Copyright 1939 by Random House, Inc. Reprinted from *The Faulkner Reader,* by permission. Random House, Inc. for excerpt from "November Surf," Copyright 1932 and renewed 1959 by Robinson Jeffers. Reprinted from *The Selected Poetry of Robinson Jeffers,* by permission of Random House, Inc. Random House, Inc. for excerpt from "Infant Boy at Midcentury: Modification of Landscape," © Copyright 1957 by Robert Penn Warren. Reprinted from *Promises: Poems 1954-1956,* by Robert Penn Warren, by permission of Random House, Inc. Charles Scribner's Sons for excerpt from "Autumn Along the Beaches," reprinted with the permission of Charles Scribner's Sons from *Poems Old and New* by John Hall Wheelock. Copyright © 1956 John Hall Wheelock. Charles Scribner's Sons for excerpt from "Death the Proud Brother" (copyright 1933 Charles Scribner's Sons; renewal copyright © 1961 Pincus Berner), reprinted with the permission of Charles Scribner's Sons from *From Death to Morning* by Thomas Wolfe. The Viking Press, Inc. for excerpt from *Travels with Charley in Search of America* by John Steinbeck. Copyright © 1961, 1962 by The Curtis Publishing Company, © 1962 by John Steinbeck. Reprinted by permission of The Viking Press, Inc. The Viking Press, Inc., for excerpt from "My City" from *St. Peter Relates an Incident* by James Weldon Johnson. Copyright 1917, 1921, 1935 by James Weldon Johnson, 1962 by Grace Nail Johnson. Reprinted by permission of The Viking Press, Inc. The World Publishing Company for excerpt from *The Color of a Great City* by Theodore Dreiser. Copyright 1923 by Boni & Liveright, Inc. Copyright 1951 by Helen Dreiser. Published by arrangement with The World Publishing Company, Cleveland and New York. Yale University Library for excerpt from Meditation LVI by Edward Taylor. Rudder Magazine for excerpt from "The Main-Sheet Song" by Thomas Fleming Day. Courtesy of Rudder Magazine, June, 1965.

COUNTRY BEAUTIFUL Magazine is published by Country Beautiful Foundation, Inc., 24198 W. Bluemound Rd., Waukesha, Wis., a nonprofit organization dedicated to strengthening and preserving the physical, cultural and moral values of America and other nations of the world.

Published simultaneously in Canada by George J. McLeod Limited, Toronto.

Library of Congress Catalog Card Number: 65-26275.

Printed in the United States of America. Color separations by Mueller Color Plate Company. Type composition by George F. Wamser, Inc., Typographers.

Lithography, Imperial Lithographing Corp., Milwaukee, Wisconsin

CONTENTS

GRAND CANYON by Thomas Moran (1837-1926).
Courtesy of Milwaukee Art Center, Layton Collection.

In its own aloof, almost contemptuous, way it is nevertheless extraordinarily beautiful — nature's ultimate achievement in that Southwestern Style which surprisingly executes great monolithic forms, sometimes sculptural and sometimes architectural. . . .

JOSEPH WOOD KRUTCH (1895-   )
From *The Desert Year*

PREFACE

THE lives of nations, like those of individuals, certainly have their constant themes but there are also periods of particular emphasis. In the late 18th century the establishment of independence and the building of a structure of freedom were to the fore. The Civil War years asserted the primacy of the issue of preserving the Union. Later decades concentrated on the peopling of a continent and the throwing up of a mighty industrial system, the reconciliation of that system with social justice, the clamorous demands of wars.

Today many of these same interests command our energies but another note is making itself heard. Now that the United States has achieved an unprecedented general affluence, the American people — especially the oncoming generation — are giving more and more attention to the quality of American civilization, the quality of all we do and say and of the whole environment in which we work and play. There is a new sense of the wisdom of Thoreau, who told us many years ago that "the highest" of human activities is to affect "the quality of the day."

Both governmental and non-governmental institutions have strikingly interested themselves in the trend. It is making itself felt in a number of highly tangible ways, whether the widespread effort to beautify the roads connecting our cities, the building of local art centers, or the drive to enrich the content of the material offered in our schools. But it is also extending into a number of intangibles, including the attitude toward the past. Cultural history, so recently a stepchild of the American mind, is coming into its own.

This volume is not only a handsome addition to the new literature; by its unique and extremely effective format of correlating the artistic and the literary past, it is likely to stimulate interest in both. *The Beauty of America in Great American Art* cannot help but be warmly welcomed by all of us who are delighted by the fresh winds of cultural concern blowing across the nation.

ERIC F. GOLDMAN

INTRODUCTION

MAN is the roamingest creature of all. He has been everywhere on earth from the deepest jungle to the highest mountain, from the depths of the sea to the frozen polar caps, and now he reaches out to the very stars themselves. Yet, as far as he may go, each man carries with him a special place, the place called home. Even in a day of shifting populations, when people move easily from place to place, making themselves at home wherever life deposits them, there is still one place special to the heart where life is richest and the sense of identity strongest. Among man's universal qualities the attachment to his homeland must certainly be one of the most pronounced.

Americans are no exception to this and have long been sensitive to the beauties and the mysteries of their native land. And in America as elsewhere the artist, whether with brush or with word, has contributed greatly to the image we hold of ourselves and our country. For it is the artist who forms man's vision and makes manifest his values. It is he who trains the eye and modulates the sentiment, and it is he who reveals the face of the nation.

During its earliest years the face of America was the face of its people alone. From the first years of colonization, throughout the 18th century, even up to the Revolution and the first decades of the young Republic, our artists were almost exclusively concerned with the painting of portraits. The face of the countryside, as expressed in landscape paintings, concerned them hardly at all, with exception being made for a few painters of topographical views and some primitive efforts at interpretive pictures now mostly lost. One of the reasons for this probably lies in security and man's fear of the unknown, for landscape is rarely painted anywhere when a visit to the countryside is dangerous. The early American years were too concerned with consolidating a tenuous grasp on the continent to take the time to stop and look at what they had conquered. The frontier was too close and its threat too imminent.

When the time came, however, that the nation began to prosper and the cities began to grow, artists began to take a new interest in what was about them. They soon discovered that what was so recently a threat was also very beautiful and very moving.

The American landscape was first discovered in the forests and fields, the rivers and mountains of the eastern hinterlands, a fact which has led to the term "Hudson River School," which refers to almost all the American landscape painters of the first half of the 19th century. There was considerable range in the approach which these artists took to the landscape and in the ways in which they chose to paint it, but generally their attitude was Romantic. Artists were concerned with the wild forces of nature which in America loomed so much larger than life. Man was only a small part of the scheme of things, generally present but rarely entirely in command. He seldom appears as more than a fisherman or farmer depicted insignificantly small somewhere in the fore or middle distance of the picture. The vast spaces of America, its immense stretches of forest, its roaring rivers and its mountains wrenched and torn by primeval forces were constant themes. They were emphasized in pictures which were often quite large in scale, and were expressive of a new awareness of nature and of a fascination with its forces and its power. To the Romantic mind of the time the controlling fact of man's existence was that he was buffeted about by these great forces and played out his life controlled by them. At the same time it was a mind which could also dream of new worlds to conquer and the American landscape in all its primeval glory provided a unique expression of the one attitude and a great physical challenge to the other.

The work of Thomas Cole (see pages 31, 38) is typical of the time in its empasis on blasted trees and endless reaches of forest and mountain wilderness. Asher B. Durand's single picture, *Kindred Spirits* (p. 14), where two small figures dwarfed by a vast forest wonder and speculate on the power of nature, contains much of the essence of this kind of painting. This attitude would continue as the nation moved west and in fact it still exerts a fascination today.

The Romantic point of view was sometimes pushed beyond the realm of natural terms onto the plane of the mystical, where the hidden forces operating behind nature were made manifest, as in the work of Albert Pinkham Ryder (pp. 70, 72) and Ralph A. Blakelock (p. 47). In these two artists the landscape becomes transformed into a strange and very personal vision.

Not all artists were so transported, however, and in an age of expanding science there were also those for whom nature was something to be observed rather than interpreted. John James Audubon (p. 34) with his magnificent studies of birds and animals from the naturalist's point of view well exemplifies the artist acting as observer which was another important thread in the fabric of the times.

In many ways the Romantic attitude of the 19th century reaches a climax in the work of George Inness (pp. 24, 32, 48). In his emphasis on a tranquil, peaceful, American scene he was continuing a tradition well established before him, which forms still another aspect of American Romantic painting. But in his interest in specific moments of time and in the consequent momentary effects of light as well as in his fascination with the manipulation of paint, he was mirroring the effects of Impressionism and paving the way for the new esthetic attitudes of the following century.

The idea of peace and abundance evident in much of the work of Inness and perhaps most appealingly treated by Edward Hicks in his many versions of the *Peaceable Kingdom* (p. 45) was a constant theme in American painting of all kinds. American democracy represented a new dream of cooperation and prosperity on earth, and artists were sensitive to its promise. The theme is seen in many a painting of rolling hills, ploughed fields and neat homesteads beneath a benign sun. The primitive artists often seem especially close to these ideals as there are many peaceful scenes of a prosperous farm or village by these untrained but often very sensitive and highly able painters.

The theme is reflected in much still life painting as well, both by the primitives and by the more sophisticated practitioners. The bounty of the fields and the richness of the harvest were the fruits of victory over man's long struggle to gain a satisfactory means of ordering his affairs and consequently, renderings of fruit and vegetables graced many an early American interior. When looking at these it should be remembered how much closer to the land than we, were even our fairly recent forebears.

By the end of the 19th century, however, still lifes became their own excuse for being in the amazing development of the "trompe l'oeil" or "fool the eye" tradition of William Michael Harnett (p. 156) and John Frederick Peto (pp. 152, 157) and a number of others who learned to paint pictures that almost looked more real than the original subject. These curious and often exquisite paintings were deliberately done to fool the observer into believing they were the actual objects and thus to display the technical skills of the artist. Although they stem from a tradition which goes back to at least the 17th century in European painting, they are, in many ways, peculiarly expressive of the American spirit. They amply state the American emphasis on practicality, its down-to-earth concern for the facts, and the nation's great interest in perfecting the skills of the artisan. That such concerns could be stated in so beautiful a fashion is also perhaps more typically American than many realize.

History played its part, too, but not as often as might be expected. True, places important in the developing history of the nation were sometimes the subject of paintings like J. Weiss' *The Home of George Washington* (p. 57), but these were fairly rare as was the true historical painting which depicted an important event. Perhaps the best known of all such American historical paintings is *Penn's Treaty with the Indians* by Benjamin West (p. 40). This event established one of those liberal and humanitarian relationships between groups of people which were and are still so much a part of the American dream. Thus the picture expresses part of the American vision, but it was painted in England by an expatriate artist working in a rather different artistic environment than the home scene, and this kind of painting did not really become an important American phenomenon until much later and indeed was never to assume a place at the center of things. American history was perhaps too much a matter of daily experience to be removed into the realm of art, or the ideas inherent in it were too abstract for the painting of the day.

Immediate activities were something else again. These, perhaps because of their very closeness, became a favorite subject of American artists. So-called "genre" painting, or subjects from everyday life, experienced a development in this country which is hardly equalled in importance elsewhere. John Neagle's *Pat Lyon at the Forge* (p. 52) is a highly unusual portrait of a craftsman at work, and was, incidentally, one of the best known pictures of its time. Artists of considerable stature, like Winslow Homer (pp.30, 58, 64, 65[2]) and Eastman Johnson (pp. 36, 55, 56) made subjects from ordinary experience the core of their work, and others like Thomas Eakins (p. 73) produced some of their best pictures along these lines. Importance of everyday life and the prominence of the Puritan virtues are blended in such pictures, which are also an expression of the classless nature of the new democracy.

The sea is another constant theme in American painting, perhaps because so many of us came across it. Some American artists were particularly at home on the sea, and Herman Melville (p. 66) and Richard Henry Dana (p. 69) find a real counterpart in such a painter as Winslow Homer. But the sea, like the land, provided material for diverse talents, from the mysticism of Ryder to the realism of William Hart (p. 62). Other artists preferred the meeting of sea and land and particularly in the 20th century, Marsden Hartley (p. 68) expressed the elemental qualities of breaking waves in pictures of monumental simplicity; Edward Hopper (p.75) found in lighthouses another expression of the lonely mood which is characteristic of all his work; and John Marin (p. 71) created moving, living expressions of the vitality of nature in hundreds of watercolors and oils of sea and surf.

As the nation moved westward the new frontier also found its painters. The Romantic attitudes earlier established by the painters of the Hudson River School formed a ready voice to speak of the newly discovered grandeur of the scenery in the far West. The work of Albert Bierstadt (pp. 80, 83, 88, 92) is amply expressive of this. If the valley of the Hudson and the forests of the Adirondacks were inducive to thoughts of the immensity of nature and the insignificance of man, how much more so the peaks of the Rockies and the valleys of the Yosemite and the Colorado. Here was a landscape to stagger the imagination, a landscape which has not to this day lost its power to awe.

There were explorers, too, who accompanied expeditions or who struck out on their own to depict the new territories unspoiled and fresh to the eyes of the men of the East. Some, like George Caleb Bingham (pp. 89, 93), became the poets of the pioneers and the recorders of that scenery only just becoming home for Americans. The cowboy too found champions in his own time. The contemporaneity of Frederic Remington's (pp. 78, 79, 81, 90) work is perhaps its most remarkable quality. Like the dime novels, Remington was able to make of the immediate stuff of life something exciting, something romantic, even if something a little fictionalized and exaggerated.

Meanwhile, back in the East, the city was coming to the fore. The artists — earlier almost exclusively preoccupied with the countryside — began in the 20th century to turn to the urban scene. The 19th century had in general only a topographical interest in depicting the city, it produced mostly views which conveyed only the facts of appearance and which were largely geographic in nature. But now the city became the wellspring of all kinds of expression, ranging from the Romanticism of earlier landscape painting and the continuing theme of genre subjects, to new subjects and new styles which in themselves expressed a civilization primarily urban in character. Reginald Marsh in *Negroes on Rockaway Beach* (p.106) exulted in crowds and in the honky-tonk atmosphere of the city's places of amusement. John Sloan (p. 112), who as much as anyone else, discovered the American city, painted its people and its places early in the century with great sympathy and so much truth that the group of painters to which he belonged was soon termed the "Ash Can School." But he was also interested in the qualities of paint itself and in the problem of constructing a picture regardless of subject matter. These were purely 20th-century preoccupations prophetic of things to come.

Others found mystery in the city, just as some had earlier found it in the landscape. Charles Burchfield's early *Rainy Night* (p. 99) has a strange, transformed quality which the city sometimes takes on and which is prophetic of a purer mysticism in his later pictures of fantasy landscapes (p. 128). Still others developed entirely new styles like nothing ever seen before, which utilized geometric shapes, highly stylized and simplified forms, having nothing to do with nature but which grew naturally within the artificial setting of the city. Lyonel Feininger transforms a *Village Street* (p. 102) into a network of lines and angles. Charles Sheeler (p. 149) and Joseph Stella (p. 113) utilize the geometry of the city itself to express its own peculiar scope and grandeur.

American landscape in our time encompasses a tremendous wealth of attitude and means of expression. Earlier in our century the Romanticism of the past once again burst forth in the peculiarly American development of Regionalism. Artists like John Steuart Curry (pp. 91[2], 116, 134, 143), Thomas Hart Benton (p. 135) and Grant Wood (p. 124) felt that art should stem from the immediate roots of the creator and that the strength of America lay in her regional loyalties. At the same time strong influences were, as ever in American painting, coming from overseas and American art was undergoing a strong dose of internationalization. As a result of this new blood from abroad, and its intermixture with native American ideas, the richness and diversity of modern American art is great indeed. It is a development exactly analogous to the mixture of old and new populations here in America to produce a more vigorous, prolific and diverse nation. The consequent spread in styles of recent American painting is very wide. From the highly selective but nevertheless visual naturalism of Andrew Wyeth (pp. 131, 132, 138) to the strongly introspective, interior landscapes of an abstractionist like Mark Tobey (pp. 115, 145, 147) is a very large step indeed, yet both have an equal validity, and both are strongly expressive of American points of view. The work of Ernest Lawson (p.122) represents a very proper kind of Impressionism, a style of French origin which quickly spread to every other civilized country including America. The expressionism of John Marin (p. 126) — the transformation of a visual image according to the dictates of the emotions — represents a European style totally transformed into a peculiarly American product, yet both are legitimate and important aspects of the development of recent American art.

Artists continue to paint America in ever more penetrating, ever more inventive ways. They continue to give us new vision, new insights and new points of view. America, which in the press of modern civilization is losing some of its natural grandeur, nevertheless will always retain a record of what once was and what once was visualized, in the enduring record of her artists.

TRACY ATKINSON
Director, Milwaukee Art Center
Milwaukee, Wisconsin

I
Early Landscapes and Village Life

(East of the Mississippi Before 1900)

To him who in the love of Nature holds
Communion with her visible forms, she speaks
A various language; for his gayer hours
She has a voice of gladness, and a smile
And eloquence of beauty, and she glides
Into his darker musings, with a mild
And healing sympathy, that steals away
Their sharpness, ere he is aware.

WILLIAM CULLEN BRYANT (1794-1878)
From "Thanatopsis"

KINDRED SPIRITS (WILLIAM CULLEN BRYANT AND THOMAS COLE)
by Asher Brown Durand (1796-1886). The New York Public Library, Astor, Lenox and
Tilden Foundations.

When the pine tosses its cones
To the song of its waterfall tones,
Who speeds to the woodland walks?
To birds and trees who talks?
Caesar of his leafy Rome,
There the poet is at home.
He goes to the river-side,—
Not hook nor line hath he;
He stands in the meadows wide,—
Nor gun nor scythe to see.

RALPH WALDO EMERSON (1803-1882)
From "Woodnotes"

VIEW FROM APPLE HILL by Samuel F. B. Morse
(1791-1872). The Clark Collection.

Transparency by Francis G. Mayer, N.Y.C.

16

LOOKING EAST FROM DENNY HILL by Ralph Earl (c. 1785-1838). Oil.
Worcester Art Museum.

The sky is hot and hazy, and the wind,

Wing-weary with its long flight from the south,

Unfelt; yet, closely scanned, yon maple leaf

With faintest motion, as one stirs in dreams,

Confesses it.

JOHN GREENLEAF WHITTIER (1807-1892)
From "Among the Hills"

Beside the river's tranquil flood

The dark and low-walled dwellings stood,

Where many a road of open land

Stretched up and down on either hand....

JOHN GREENLEAF WHITTIER (1807-1892)
From "Pentucket"

PEACEFUL VILLAGE by unknown American primitive artist about 1850.
From the Collection of Edgar William and Bernice Chrysler Garbisch.

And towns shoot up, and fertile
   realms are tilled;
... [where] the full region leads
New colonies forth, that toward the
   western seas
Spread, like a rapid flame among
   the autumnal trees.

WILLIAM CULLEN BRYANT (1794-1878)
From "The Ages"

20

POESTENKILL, NEW YORK by Joseph H. Hidley (1830-1872). Oil on wood.
The Metropolitan Museum of Art, gift of Edgar William and Bernice Chrysler Garbisch, 1963.

RIP VAN WINKLE AT NICHOLAS VEDDER'S TAVERN by John Quidor (1801-1881).
Courtesy, Museum of Fine Arts, Boston.

For a long time [Rip Van Winkle] used to console himself, when driven from home, by frequenting a kind of perpetual club of sages, philosophers, and other idle personages of the village; which held its sessions on a bench before a small inn. . . .

The opinions of this junto were completely controlled by Nicholas Vedder, a patriarch of the village, and landlord of the inn. . . .

WASHINGTON IRVING (1783-1859)
From "Rip Van Winkle"

OVERLEAF

As I spoke, beneath my feet
The ground-pine curled its pretty wreath,
Running over the club-moss burrs;
I inhaled the violet's breath;
Around me stood the oaks and firs;
Pine-cones and acorns lay on the ground;
Over me soared the eternal sky,
Full of light and of deity. . . .

RALPH WALDO EMERSON (1803-1882)
From "Each and All"

CATSKILL MOUNTAINS by George Inness (1825-1894). Oil.
Courtesy of The Art Institute of Chicago, Edward B. Butler Collection.

24

Niagara Falls! By what mysterious power is it that millions and millions, are drawn from all parts of the world, to gaze upon Niagara Falls? There is no mystery about the thing itself. . . . Its power to excite reflection, and emotion, is its great charm.

ABRAHAM LINCOLN (1809-1865)
Address, c. September 25-30, 1848

VIEW OF NIAGARA by John Trumbull (1756-1843)
Wadsworth Atheneum, Hartford, Conn.

DELAWARE WATER GAP VILLAGE by Louis Michel Eilshemius (1864-1941) Oil.
The Metropolitan Museum of Art, Arthur H. Hearn Fund. 1932.

O past! O happy life! O song of joy!

In the air, in the woods, over fields . . .

WALT WHITMAN (1819-1892)
From "Out of the Cradle Endlessly Rocking"

OVERLEAF

The land is full of harvests and green meads;

Streams numberless, that many a fountain feeds,

Shine, disembowered, and give to sun and breeze

Their virgin waters. . . .

WILLIAM CULLEN BRYANT (1794-1878)
From "The Ages"

RIVER SCENE by John Frederick Kensett (1816-1872).
The Metropolitan Museum of Art, bequest of Collis P. Huntington, 1925.

28

Here, life the undiminished man demands;

New faculties stretch out to meet new wants;

What Nature asks, that Nature also grants....

JAMES RUSSELL LOWELL (1819-1891)
From "The Pioneer"

WOODSMAN AND FALLEN TREE by Winslow Homer (1836-1910).
Museum of Fine Arts, Boston.

THE OXBOW by Thomas Cole (1801-1848). The Metropolitan Museum of Art, gift of Mrs. Russell Sage, 1908.

An earth, where gushing springs and corn for bread
By me at every season should be given;
Yet not the water or the bread that now
Supplies their tables with its daily food,
But they should gather fruit from every bough,
Such as Thou givest me, and call it good. . . .

JONES VERY (1813-1880)
From "The Earth"

OVERLEAF

PEACE AND PLENTY by George Inness (1825-1894). The Metropolitan Museum of Art, gift of George A. Hearn.

Ferruginous Thrush

To live where you would hear the first brown thrasher!

First, perchance, you have a glimpse of one's ferruginous long brown back,

instantly lost amid the shrub oaks, and are uncertain if it was the thrasher,

or one of the other thrushes; and your uncertainty lasts commonly a day or two,

until its rich and varied strain is heard.

HENRY DAVID THOREAU (1817-1862)
From his Journals

BROWN THRASHER by John James Audubon (1785-1851). National Audubon Society.

CORNHUSKING BEE by Eastman Johnson (1824-1906). Oil.
Courtesy of The Art Institute of Chicago.

When the farmers made "bees," as they did a generation or two ago much more than they do now, a picturesque element was added. There was the stone bee, the husking bee, the "raising," the "moving" [bee]. . . .

JOHN BURROUGHS (1837-1921)
From *In the Catskills*

OVERLEAF

Nature loves such woods, and places her seal upon them. . . . The soil is marrowy and full of innumerable forests. Standing in those fragrant aisles, I . . . am awed by the deep and inscrutable processes of life going on so silently about me.

JOHN BURROUGHS (1837-1921)
From *In the Catskills*

THE CATSKILL MOUNTAINS by Thomas Cole (1801-1848). Cleveland Museum of Art.

To sing of Wars, of Captains, and of Kings,

Of Cities founded, Common-wealths begun,

For my mean pen are too superiour things:

Or how they all or each their dates have run,

Let Poets and Historians set these forth,

My obscure Lines shall not so dim their worth.

ANNE BRADSTREET (c. 1612-1672)
From "The Prologue"

PENN'S TREATY WITH THE INDIANS by Benjamin West (1738-1820).
Courtesy of the Pennsylvania Academy of the Fine Arts.

AMERICAN FARM SCENE by N. Currier (1813-1888) after F. F. Palmer.
Lithograph. Courtesy of The Old Print Shop Inc.

. . . Man may be civilized, in some degree, without great progress in manu-factures and with little commerce with his distant neighbors. But without the cultivation of the earth, he is, in all countries, a savage. Until he gives up the chase, and fixes himself in some place and seeks a living from the earth, he is a roaming barbarian. When tillage begins, other arts follow. The farmers, therefore, are the founders of human civilization.

DANIEL WEBSTER (1782-1852)
January 14, 1840

THROUGH SNOW-CLAD HILLS AND VALLEYS by Gardner Symons (1863-1930).
Collection City Art Museum of Saint Louis.

The sun that brief December day

Rose cheerless over hills of gray,

And, darkly circled, gave at noon

A sadder light than waning moon.

JOHN GREENLEAF WHITTIER (1807-1892)
From "Snowbound"

42

When breezes are soft and skies are fair,

I steal an hour from study and care,

And hie me away to the woodland scene...

WILLIAM CULLEN BRYANT (1794-1878)
From "Green River"

SCENE IN THE CATSKILL MOUNTAINS by Frederic E. Church (1826-1900).
Walker Art Center.

Visited the woods again yesterday. . . . It was a superb day without a cloud,
With a soft wind — one of those strong, positive days — a he-day —
impregnating the earth with the generative principle of sunshine.

JOHN BURROUGHS (1837-1921)
From his Journals

DEER, MOUNT STORM PARK, CINCINNATI by T. Worthington Whittredge (1820-1910).
Oil. Worcester Art Museum.

THE PEACEABLE KINGDOM by Edward Hicks (1780-1849).
New York State Historical Association, Cooperstown, New York.

Thou art the Tree of Life in Paradise,

  Whose lively branches are with Clusters hung

Of Lovely fruits, and Flowers more sweet than spice.

  Bende down to us, and doe outshine the sun.

  Delightfull unto God, doe man rejoyce

  The pleasant'st fruits in all Gods Paradise.

EDWARD TAYLOR (c. 1645-1729)
From "Sacremental Meditations"

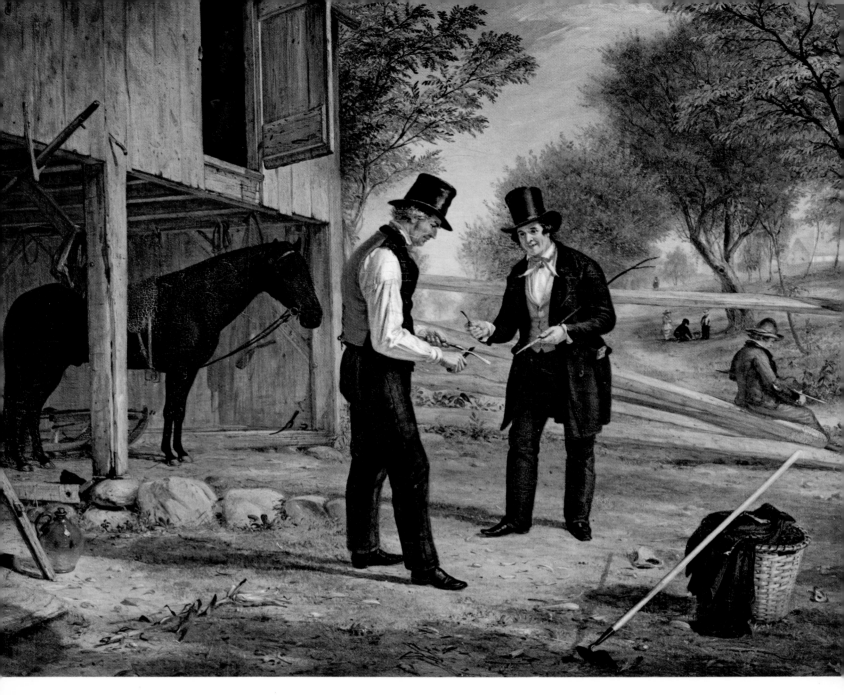

COMING TO THE POINT by William Sidney Mount (1807-1868).
The New-York Historical Society.

"A cat in gloves catches no mice."

"Diligence is the mother of good-luck."

"God gives all things to industry."

BENJAMIN FRANKLIN (1706-1790)
Poor Richard's sayings from "A Way to Wealth"

As a pale phantom with a lamp
  Ascends some ruin's haunted stair,
So glides the moon along the damp
  Mysterious chambers of the air.

Now hidden in cloud, and now revealed,
  As if this phantom, full of pain,
Were by the crumbling walls concealed,
  And at the windows seen again.

HENRY WADSWORTH LONGFELLOW (1807-1882)
From "Moonlight"

MOONLIGHT by Ralph A. Blakelock (1847-1919). Oil. The Brooklyn Museum.

AUTUMN OAKS by George Inness (1825-1894).
The Metropolitan Museum of Art, gift of George I. Seney, 1887.

Come let's roam the breezy pastures,

Where the freest zephyrs blow,

Batten on the oak tree's rustle,

And the pleasant insect bustle,

Dripping with the streamlet's flow.

HENRY DAVID THOREAU (1817-1862)
From "The Breeze's Invitation"

When Winter fringes every bough
With his fantastic wreath,
And puts the seal of silence now
Upon the leaves beneath. . . .

HENRY DAVID THOREAU (1817-1862)
From "When Winter fringes every bough"

FROSTBITTEN WOOD AND FIELD by John Francis Murphy (1853-1921). Oil.
Courtesy of the Smithsonian Institution, Freer Gallery of Art, Washington, D.C.

The constancy of this serenely cold weather is one of the greatest blessings which seldom fail us. More to the southward their winters are often interrupted by thaws and rains which are unfavorable to transportation....

J. HECTOR ST. JOHN DE CRÈVECŒUR (1731-1813)
From "A Snow Storm As It Affects the American Farmer"

AMERICAN LANDSCAPE by L. Whitney (? - ?). Oil. Collection of the Newark Museum. Purchase 1931, Felix Fuld Bequest.

TWILIGHT — MAY by Dwight Tryon (1849-1925). Oil on wood panel. Courtesy of the Smithsonian Institution, Freer Gallery of Art, Washington, D.C.

Quiet the longing
Of my hands that yearn,
As you fold the flower
And hush the fern.

HAZEL HALL (1886-1924)
From "Twilight"

The smith, a mighty man is he,

    With large and sinewy hands;

And the muscles of his brawny arms

    Are strong as iron bands.

HENRY WADSWORTH LONGFELLOW (1807-1882)
From "The Village Blacksmith"

PAT LYON AT THE FORGE by John B. Neagle (1796-1866).
Courtesy of the Boston Athenaeum.

Near to the bank of the river, o'ershadowed

by oaks, from whose branches

Garlands of Spanish moss and of mystic

mistletoe flaunted. . . .

HENRY WADSWORTH LONGFELLOW (1807-1882)
From "Evangeline"

THE LAND OF EVANGELINE by Joseph R. Meeker (1827-1889).
Collection City Art Museum of Saint Louis.

My boy had not a great deal to do with schools after his docile childhood. When he began to run wild with the other boys he preferred their savage freedom; and he got out of going to school by most of the devices they used. He had never quite the hardihood to play truant, but he was subject to sudden attacks of sickness, which came on about school-time and went off towards the middle of the forenoon or afternoon in a very strange manner.

WILLIAM DEAN HOWELLS (1837-1920)
From *A Boy's Town*

OLD STAGE COACH by Eastman Johnson (1824-1906).
Courtesy of Milwaukee Art Center, Layton Collection.

We will sing one song for the old Kentucky Home,

For the old Kentucky Home far away.

STEPHEN COLLINS FOSTER (1826-1864)
From "My Old Kentucky Home"

OLD KENTUCKY HOME by Eastman Johnson (1824-1906). The New-York Historical Society.

Relying on its kindness in this as in other things, and actuated by that fervent love towards it which is so natural to a man who views in it the native soil of himself and his progenitors for several generations; I anticipate with pleasing expectation that retreat in which I promise myself to realize, without alloy, the sweet enjoyment of partaking in the midst of my fellow citizens, the benign influence of good laws under a free government. . . .

GEORGE WASHINGTON (1732-1799)
From "Farewell Address"

PROUT'S NECK, BREAKING WAVE by Winslow Homer (1836-1910). Water color.
Courtesy of The Art Institute of Chicago, Mr. and Mrs. Martin A. Ryerson Collection.

II
The Sea and the Coast

Some lucky day each November great waves awake and are drawn

Like smoking mountains bright from the west

And come and cover cliff with white violent cleanness. . . .

ROBINSON JEFFERS (1887-1962)
From "November Surf"

YACHT RACE by Maurice Prendergast (1859-1924). Water color.
Courtesy of The Art Institute of Chicago, Watson F. Blair purchase prize.

Rushing along on a narrow reach,
Our rival under the lee,
The wind falls foul of the weather leach,
And the jib flaps fretfully.

THOMAS FLEMING DAY (1861-1927)
From "The Main-Sheet Song"

Since as in night's deck-watch ye show,
Why, lads, so silent here to me,
Your watchmate of times long ago?

Once, for all the darkling sea,
You your voices raised how clearly....

HERMAN MELVILLE (1819-1891)
From *John Marr and Other Sailors, with Some Sea-Pieces*

HEAVY THE OAR TO HIM WHO IS TIRED, HEAVY THE COAT, HEAVY THE SEA
by Ivan Albright (1897-   ). Oil. Courtesy of The Art Institute of Chicago,
gift of Mr. and Mrs. Earle Ludgin.

61

SEASHORE-MORNING by William Hart (1823-1894).
The Metropolitan Museum of Art, gift of the sons of William Paton, 1909.

There lies a somnolent lake
Under a noiseless sky,
Where never the mornings break
Nor the evenings die.

TRUMBULL STICKNEY (1874-1904)
From "In the Past"

EIGHT BELLS by Winslow Homer (1836-1910). Addison Gallery of American Art,
Phillips Academy, Andover, Massachusetts.

*...The marvel of it! That tiny men should live and breathe and work, and
drive so frail a contrivance of wood and cloth through so tremendous an
elemental strife.*

JACK LONDON (1876-1916)
From *The Sea-Wolf*

THE HERRING NET by Winslow Homer (1836-1910). Oil.
Courtesy of The Art Institute of Chicago, Mr. and Mrs. Martin A. Ryerson Collection.

64

"Wouldst thou" — so the helmsman answered,

    "Learn the secret of the sea?

Only those who brave its dangers

    Comprehend its mystery!"

HENRY WADSWORTH LONGFELLOW (1807-1882)
From "The Secret of the Sea"

THE GALE by
Winslow Homer (1836-1910).
Oil. Worcester Art Museum.

INCIDENTS IN WHALE FISHING by Frederic Martens (19th Century) after a painting by
Ambrose Louis Garneray (1783-1857). Engraving. Courtesy of The Old Print Shop Inc.

Not the raw recruit, marching from the bosom of his wife into the fever heat of his first battle; not the dead man's ghost encountering the first unknown phantom in the other world;—neither of these can feel stranger and stronger emotions than that man does, who for the first time finds himself pulling into the charmed, churned circle of the hunted Sperm Whale.

HERMAN MELVILLE (1819-1891)
From *Moby Dick*

THE CLIPPER SHIP "NIGHTINGALE" by N. Currier (1813-1888). Lithograph.
From *Currier & Ives: Printmakers to the American People* by Harry T. Peters,
published by Doubleday, Inc.

Splendid now in my dream

The snows of the clipper gleam,

Tower of marble, glorious, tall in the sun —

Hurling south to the hurricanes of the Horn.

GEORGE STERLING (1869-1926)
From "Sails"

But now, our boat climbs — hesitates — drops —

climbs — hesitates — crawls back —

climbs — hesitates —

O be swift —

We have known you wanted us.

H.D. (Hilda Doolittle) (1886-1961)
From "The Helmsman"

NORTHERN SEASCAPE by Marsden Hartley (1877-1943). Oil.
Courtesy of Milwaukee Art Center.

THE RISING OF A THUNDERSTORM AT SEA by Washington Allston (1779-1843).
Courtesy, Museum of Fine Arts, Boston.

*I felt the vessel pitching at her anchor, and the chain surging and snapping.
. . . The mate called out, down the scuttle, "Tumble up here, men! tumble
up! before she drags her anchor." We were on deck in an instant. "Lay
aloft and loose the topsails!" Springing into the rigging, I saw that the
Ayacucho's topsails were loosed, and heard her crew singing-out at the
sheets as they were hauling them home.*

RICHARD HENRY DANA, JR. (1815-1882)
From *Two Years Before the Mast*

THE WASTE OF WATERS IS THEIR FIELD by Albert Pinkham Ryder (1847-1917).
Oil on panel. The Brooklyn Museum.

Where leap the long Atlantic swells
  In foam-streaked stretch of hill and dale,
Where shrill the north-wind demon yells,
  And flings the spindrift down the gale....

JOSEPH C. LINCOLN (1870-1944)
From *"The Cod-Fisher"*

The bay was full of sparks of Autumn light,
Fair-weather waves ran turning over white.

ROBERT P. TRISTRAM COFFIN (1892-1955)
From "Mainland-Woman's Return"

GRAY AND GREEN: THE SILVER SEA by James Abbott McNeill Whistler (1834-1903).
Oil. Courtesy of The Art Institute of Chicago, Potter Palmer Collection.

70

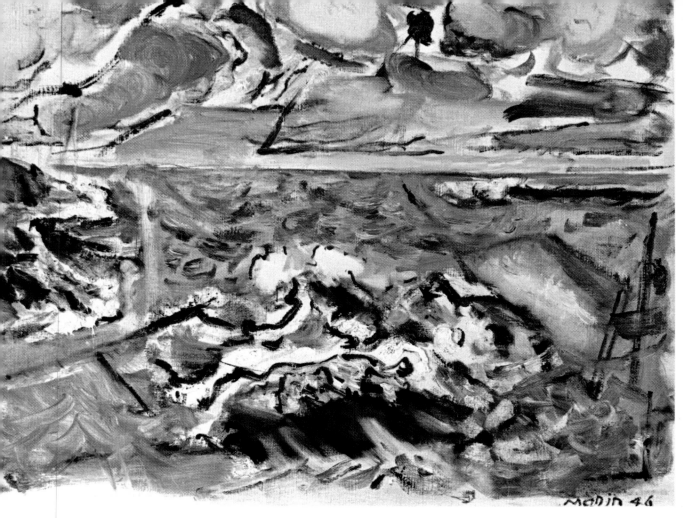

MOVEMENT — SEA AND SKY by John Marin (1870-1953). Oil. Lane Foundation, Leominster, Mass.

. . . O mariner, dost thou never feel
The grandeur of thy office,
*   — to control*
The keel that cuts the ocean like
*   a knife*
And leaves behind it like a seam
In the great shining garment
*   of the world?*

OLIVER WENDELL HOLMES (1809-1894)
From "A Sea Dialogue"

THE TOILERS OF THE SEA by Albert Pinkham Ryder (1847-1917).
The Metropolitan Museum of Art, George A. Hearn Fund.

I must forth again to-morrow!
With the sunset I must be
Hull down on the trail of rapture
In the wonder of the sea.

RICHARD HOVEY (1864-1900)
From "The Sea Gipsy"

STARTING OUT AFTER RAIL by Thomas Eakins
(1844-1916). Water color. Wichita Art Museum,
Roland P. Murdock Collection, Wichita, Kansas.

Autumn is on the wind; the chilly air
   Is wide and vacant, the pale waters seem
Paler and lonelier — lonely and bare,
   The tawney beaches fading like a dream.

JOHN HALL WHEELOCK (1886-   )
From "Autumn Along the Beaches"

THE SAND TEAM by George Wesley Bellows (1882-1925). Oil. The Brooklyn Museum.

73

This is a salt steep-cobbled town

    where every morning the men go down

    to breathe the sun-wet sea. . . .

FRANCES FROST (1905-1959)
From "Sea Town"

GLOUCESTER WHARF by Stuart Davis (1894-1964). Gouache.
Courtesy Milwaukee Art Center.

LIGHTHOUSE AT TWO LIGHTS by Edward Hopper (1882-   ).
The Metropolitan Museum of Art, Hugo Kastor Fund, 1962.

The rocky ledge runs far into the sea,
  And on its outer point, some miles away,
The Lighthouse lifts its massive masonry,
  A pillar of fire by night, of cloud by day.

HENRY WADSWORTH LONGFELLOW (1807-1882)
From "The Lighthouse"

FUR TRAPPERS RENDEZVOUS by Alfred Jacob Miller (1810-1874).

III
The Western Frontier

Tent and tipis spread along the creeks. Large herds of horses and mules grazed the plain. Every day or so another little group came in, from as far away as the Three Forks, or South Park, or Brown's Hole. They had the winter's histories to exchange, the absent and the killed to account for, fellowship to renew.

BERNARD DE VOTO (1897-1955)
From *Across the Wide Missouri*

HOWL OF THE WEATHER by Frederic Remington (1861-1909).
Remington Art Memorial, Ogdensburg, N.Y.

Wail, wind of the bitter breath,

... it is woe you bring,

Blowing out from forbidden worlds,

From icy caverns beneath old glaciers....

ALICE HENSON ERNST
From "Ya-Ihl's Song to the North Wind"

Thou shalt not grow discouraged, nor think of going home before thou hast made thy "pile," because thou hast not "struck a lead," not found a "rich crevice" . . . lest in going home thou shalt leave four dollars a day, and go to work, ashamed, at fifty cents, and serve thee right. . . .

JAMES M. HUTCHINGS (1820-1902)
From Commandment VII of "The Miners' Ten Commandments"

THE PROSPECTORS by Frederic Remington (1861-1909). Oil.
The Whitney Gallery of Western Art, Cody, Wyoming.

I turn round and round irresolute sometimes for a quarter of an hour, until I decide, for the thousandth time, that I will walk into the southwest or west. Eastward I go only by force, but westward I go free. . . . I believe that the forest which I see in the western horizon stretches uninterruptedly toward the setting sun, and there are no towns or cities in it of enough consequence to disturb me. . . . I am leaving the city more and more and withdrawing into the wilderness. I should not lay so much stress on this fact if I did not believe that something like this is the prevailing tendency of my countrymen.

HENRY DAVID THOREAU (1817-1862)
From "Walking"

WIND RIVER MOUNTAIN (Former territory of Wyoming, now Nebraska) by Albert Bierstadt (1830-1902). Oil. Courtesy Milwaukee Art Center.

THE OUTLIER by Frederic Remington (1861-1909). Remington
Art Memorial, Ogdensburg, N.Y.

Look as they rise, rise

Over the line where sky meets the earth;

Pleiades!

Lo! They ascending, come to guide us,

Leading us safely, keeping us one;

Pleiades,

Teach us to be, like you, united.

PAWNEE
"Song of the Pleiades"

THE PURSUIT by Arthur F. Tait (1819-1905). Oil.
Collection of Mr. and Mrs. Edward S. Tallmadge.

[Horses] plowed the land; packed the provisions; with the help of their half brother, the mule, they did most of the freighting; carried the mail; herded the cattle; fought the Indians. . . . Pioneering without horses would have been unthinkable.

HERMAN OLIVER (1885-   )
From *Gold and Cattle Country*
Binfords & Mort, Publishers

The forests of America, however slighted by man, must have been a great delight to God; for they were the best He ever planted.

JOHN MUIR (1838-1914)
From *The American Forests*

GIANT REDWOODS OF CALIFORNIA by Albert Bierstadt (1830-1920).
Permanent Collection of The Berkshire Museum.

LEWIS AND CLARK MEETING FLATHEAD INDIANS by Charles M.
Russell (1864-1926). Mural. Montana Historical Society.

Then we pursued the course of the stream for three miles, till it emptied into a river from the east. In the wide valley at their junction, we discovered a large camp of Indians. When we reached them and alighted from our horses we were received with great cordiality.

MERIWETHER LEWIS (1774-1809)
and WILLIAM CLARK (1770-1838)
From *Journals of the Expedition*

A BUFFALO HUNT by Charles M. Russell (1864-1926). Courtesy Kennedy Galleries, Inc.

BUFFALO HUNT by Richard Lorenz (1858-1915). Oil. Courtesy of Milwaukee Art Center.

In a moment I was in the midst of a cloud, half suffocated by the dust and stunned by the trampling of the flying herd; but I was drunk with the chase and cared for nothing but the buffalo.

FRANCIS PARKMAN (1823-1893)
From *The California and The Oregon Trail*

The escape of the Cheyennes from the hungry south, with other tribes trying it too, and the flight of the last few buffaloes to the breaks, or across the Rio Grande, these were symbols of an era's passing, and the hunters of it vanished like the shadows of the great herds.

MARI SANDOZ (1901-   )
From *The Buffalo Hunters*

LAST OF THE BUFFALO by Albert Bierstadt (1830-1902). The Whitney Gallery of Western Art, Cody, Wyoming.

RAFTSMEN PLAYING CARDS by George Caleb Bingham (1811-1879).
Collection City Art Museum of Saint Louis.

They sung, "Jolly, Jolly Raftsman's the Life for Me," with a rousing chorus, and then . . . they talked about how Ohio water didn't like to mix with Mississippi water.

MARK TWAIN (SAMUEL CLEMENS) (1835-1910)
From *Life on the Mississippi*

AIDING A COMRADE by Frederic Remington (1861-1909). Oil.
Hogg Brothers Collection, The Museum of Fine Arts, Houston.

*Cowboy, cattleman, cowpuncher, it matters not what name others have given
him, he has remained — himself. . . . He never dreamed he was a hero.*

EMERSON HOUGH (1857-1923)
From *The Story of the Cowboy*

*The sun up-sprang,
Its light swept the plain like a sea
Of golden water, and the blue-gray dome
That soared above the settler's shack
Was lighted into magical splendor.*

HAMLIN GARLAND (1860-1940)
From *Prairie Songs*

OKLAHOMA LAND RUSH by John Steuart Curry (1897-1946). Mural.
Courtesy of U. S. Department of the Interior.

Twelve o'clock. There went up a roar that drowned the crack of the soldiers' musketry as they fired in the air as the signal of noon and the start of the Run. . . . The thousands surged over the Line. It was like water going over a broken dam. The rush had started, and it was devil take the hindmost. We swept across the prairie in a cloud of black and red dust. . . .

EDNA FERBER (1887-   )
From *Cimarron*

THE HOMESTEAD by John Steuart Curry (1897-1946). Mural.
Courtesy of U.S. Department of the Interior.

Sell a country! Why not sell the air, the clouds and the great sea, as well as the earth? Did not the Great Spirit make them all for the use of his children?

TECUMSEH (1768?-1813)

ISLAND IN A SOUND by Albert Bierstadt (1830 - 1902). Oil. Courtesy of The Art Institute of Chicago, Charles H. and Mary F. S. Worcester Collection.

LANDSCAPE by George Caleb Bingham (1811-1879).
Collection City Art Museum of Saint Louis.

Land of large merciful-hearted skies,
   Big bounties, rich increase,
Green rests for Trade's blood-shotten eyes,
   For o'er-beat brain's surcease,
For Love the dear woods' sympathies,
   For Grief the wise woods' peace. . . .

SIDNEY LANIER (1842-1881)
From "Psalm of the West"

CITY LIGHTS by Richard Florsheim (1916-   ).
Courtesy of the artist.

Below, straight streets, monotonous,
   From north and south, from east and west,
Stretch glittering; and luminous
   Above, one tower tops the rest
   And holds aloft man's constant quest. . . .

AMY LOWELL (1874-1925)
From "New York at Night"

IV
The American City: Yesterday and Today

NEW YORK NIGHT by Georgia O'Keeffe (1887-   ).
Nebraska Art Association, gift of Mr. and Mrs. Frank H. Woods
in memory of Thomas C. Woods, Sr.

I never return to this wonderful city [New York] without being entertained and impressed afresh. New York is full of types and figures and curious social idiosyncrasies....

HENRY JAMES (1843-1916)
From a letter to George du Maurier

THE MALL — CENTRAL PARK by Maurice Prendergast (1859-1924).
Water color. Courtesy of The Art Institute of Chicago, Olivia Shaler Swan Collection.

I am pleased with this city; it is beautifully situated. . . . The town has a romantic appearance. . . . Annapolis appears to me to be a most economical and pleasing place of residence for those who have no particular profession or commercial pursuit. . . .

DAVID B. WARDEN (1772-1845)
From his Journal

FRANCIS STREET, ANNAPOLIS by Francis Blackwell Mayer (1827-1899).
The Metropolitan Museum of Art, Rogers Fund, 1939.

RAINY NIGHT by Charles E. Burchfield (1893-   )
From the permanent collection of the Fine Arts Society of San Diego.

As I lie roofed in, screened in,

From the pattering rain —

As I lie

Snug and dry,

And hear the birds complain.

HARRIET MONROE (1860-1936)
From "On the Porch"

VILLAGE STREET by Lyonel Feininger (1871-1956).
Oil. Courtesy of The Art Institute of Chicago,
gift of Mr. and Mrs. Sigmund Kunstadter.

His mind, fallen inward, stirs no more,
only the house rises;
count the bricks, the stones
and estimate their power
against wind and rain, time and dissolution.

HORACE GREGORY (1898-   )
From "Homestead"

Go into any one of these areas and you will
encounter a civilization that is as strange
and un-American as if it were not included
in this land at all. Pushcarts and market-
stalls are among the most distinctive
features. . . . There is an atmosphere of
crowdedness and poverty which goes with both.

THEODORE DREISER (1871-1945)
From *The Color of a Great City*

THE BUTCHER CART by George Benjamin Luks (1867-1933). Oil.
Courtesy of The Art Institute of Chicago, Friends of American Art Collection.

HOLIDAY ON THE HUDSON by George Benjamin Luks (1867-1933). Oil.
The Cleveland Museum of Art, Hinman B. Hurlbut Collection.

The river and bay scenery, all about New York island, any time of a fine day . . . — the myriad of white sail'd schooners, sloops, skiffs . . . — the prospect off toward Staten Island, or down the Narrows, or the other way up the Hudson — what refreshment of spirit such sights and experiences gave me years ago (and many a time since)!

WALT WHITMAN (1819-1892)
From *Specimen Days*

Snow and stars, the same as ever
In the days when I was young, —
But their silver song, ah never,
Never now is sung!

WILLIAM WINTER (1836-1917)
From "Age"

CENTRAL PARK, WINTER by William J. Glackens (1870-1938).
The Metropolitan Museum of Art, George A. Hearn Fund.

In the Negroes of the quarter

Pressure of the blood is slightly higher

In the quarter of the Negroes

Where black shadows move like shadows

Cut from shadows cut from shade

LANGSTON HUGHES (1902-   )
From "Jazztet Muted"

NEGROES ON ROCKAWAY BEACH by Reginald Marsh (1898-1954).
Egg tempera on composition board. Collection of the Whitney Museum of
American Art, gift of Mr. and Mrs. Albert Hackett.

THE BOWERY by Reginald Marsh (1898-1954). Tempera on masonite.
The Metropolitan Museum of Art, Arthur H. Hearn Fund.

But, ah! Manhattan's sights and sounds, her smells,
Her crowds, her throbbing force, the thrill that comes
From being of her a part, her subtle spells,
Her shining towers, her avenues, her slums. . . .

JAMES WELDON JOHNSON (1871-1938)
From "My City"

Transparency by Francis G. Mayer, N.Y.C.

SPRING IN CENTRAL PARK by Adolf Dehn (1895-   ). Water color.
The Metropolitan Museum of Art, Fletcher Fund, 1941.

*I found myself, in May and June, getting
into [Central Park] whenever I could. . . .
The crowd, in the happiest seasons, at
favoring hours . . . has, for what it is, none
but the mildest action on the nerves. The
nerves are too grateful, the intention of
beauty everywhere too insistent. . . .*

HENRY JAMES (1843-1916)
From *The American Scene*

The face of the night, the heart of the dark, the tongue of the flame — I had known all things that lived or stirred or worked below her destiny. I was the child of night, a son among her mighty family, and I knew all that moved within the hearts of men who loved the night.

THOMAS WOLFE (1900-1938)
From "Death the Proud Brother"

NIGHTHAWKS by Edward Hopper (1882-   ). Oil. Courtesy of The Art Institute of Chicago, Friends of American Art Collection.

I move an alien in the changing street;

I see no faces and I hear no sound,

Neither the wheeling pomp of the effete,

Nor haggard agony, the anxious round,

Of those who slink along the bitter ground.

MAX EASTMAN (1883-   )
From "The City"

MANHATTAN by Loren MacIver (1909-   ). Oil.
ART:USA, The Johnson Collection of Contemporary American Paintings.

Adamant, though smirched, the snow refused

Solar orders that came confused

In the intersecting shadows of

Buildings that despoiled the sun's right

To shine there forcefully and to shine bright

MERRILL MOORE (1903-1957)
From "Streets in Dislocation, Stolid Snow . . ."

BACKYARDS, GREENWICH VILLAGE by John Sloan (1871-1951). Whitney Museum.

112

THE BRIDGE by Joseph Stella (1880-1946).
Oil. Collection of the Newark Museum.
Purchase 1937, Felix Fuld Bequest.

And Thee, across the harbor, silver-paced
As though the sun took step of thee, yet left
Some motion ever unspent in thy stride,—
Implicitly thy freedom staying thee?

HART CRANE (1899-1932)
From "The Bridge"

113

FROM WILLIAMSBURG BRIDGE by Edward Hopper (1882-   ). Oil.
The Metropolitan Museum of Art, George A. Hearn Fund, 1937.

Hence the houses of this district, having had a thousand dwellers, should have a thousand tales to tell, mostly dull ones no doubt; but it would be strange if there could not be found a ghost or two in the wake of all those vagrant guests.

WILLIAM SIDNEY PORTER ("O. Henry") (1862-1910)
From "The Furnished Room"

114

SAN FRANCISCO STREET by Mark Tobey (1890-   ).
Collection of The Detroit Institute of Arts.

Like all special cities of the world, San Francisco is a many-textured thing, its light and shadows constantly shifting. It grows and changes, landmarks moving and tumbling, and still it remains uniquely San Francisco. . . .

HERB CAEN (1916-   )
From *Our San Francisco*

I remembered now that I had been told Wisconsin is a lovely state, but the telling had not prepared me. It was a magic day.

JOHN STEINBECK (1902-   )
From *Travels with Charley in Search of America*

WISCONSIN LANDSCAPE by John Steuart Curry (1897-1946).
The Metropolitan Museum of Art, George A. Hearn Fund, 1942.

V
The American Landscape in the 20th Century

My country has the Winter for its year.

I know the snow is never far away. . . .

ROBERT P. TRISTRAM COFFIN (1892-1955)
From "Winter Is My Year"

What death more wonderful

Than day's in winter?

All the cold west burns,

Burns to be near its insatiable lover,

The dark.

MARK VAN DOREN (1894-   )
From "December Setting"

ICEBOUND by Willard L. Metcalf (1858-1925). Oil. Courtesy of The Art Institute of Chicago, Walter H. Schulze Memorial Collection.

When I look out upon the world after the first snowfall I always think that it is brand new, another kind of genesis, innocent and waiting for new and better transcriptions. Not only is the clutter and litter of autumn hidden and simplified, but the whole scene of man's argument and confusion is cleansed and made briefly immaculate. All things are possible again. Even wisdom, Even understanding.

HAL BORLAND (1900-   )
From "The Whisper of Winter"

MOUNT EQUINOX, WINTER by Rockwell Kent (1882-   ). Oil.
Courtesy of The Art Institute of Chicago, gift of Gertrude V. Whitney.

WINTER ON THE RIVER by Ernest Lawson (1873-1939). Oil.
Collection of the Whitney Museum of American Art.

Winter is a study in half tones, and one must have an eye for them, or go lonely. Trees, skies, and even the black, white and gray and rufous colors of winter birds and little mammals, all are subdued, modest, economical of a lofty beauty.

DONALD CULROSS PEATTIE (1898-1964)
From *An Almanac for Moderns*

122

But Winter has yet brighter scenes — he boasts

Splendors beyond what gorgeous Summer knows;

Or Autumn with his many fruits, and woods

All flushed with many hues. Come when the rains

Have glazed the snow and clothed the trees with ice. . . .

WILLIAM CULLEN BRYANT (1794-1878)
From "A Winter Piece"

WINTER by Rockwell Kent (1882-　　). Oil.
The Metropolitan Museum of Art, George A. Hearn Fund.

A hurry of hoofs in a village street,
A shape in the moonlight, a bulk
  in the dark,
And beneath, from the pebbles, in
  passing, a spark
Struck out by a steed flying fearless
  and fleet:
That was all! And yet, through the
  gloom and the light,
The fate of a nation was riding
  that night. . . .

HENRY WADSWORTH LONGFELLOW
(1807-1882) From "Paul Revere's Ride"

124

MIDNIGHT RIDE OF PAUL REVERE by Grant Wood (1892-1942).
The Metropolitan Museum of Art, The Arthur H. Hearn Fund, 1950.

SPRING NO. 1 by John Marin (1870-1953).
Courtesy of The Phillips Collection.

Spring is like a perhaps hand
(which comes carefully
out of Nowhere)arranging
a window, into which people look(while
people stare
arranging and changing placing
carefully there a strange
thing and a known thing here)and

changing everything carefully

E. E. CUMMINGS (1894-1962)
From "Spring is like a perhaps hand"

126

At midnight, in the month of June,

I stand beneath the mystic moon.

An opiate vapor, dewy, dim,

Exhales from out her golden rim,

EDGAR ALLAN POE (1809-1849)
From "The Sleeper"

DIRGE IN SPRING by Arthur B. Davies (1862-1928). Oil. Courtesy of The Art Institute of Chicago, Mr. and Mrs. Martin A. Ryerson Collection.

SPRING by Ben Shahn (1898-   ). Albright-Knox Art Gallery, Room of Contemporary Art Fund, Buffalo, New York.

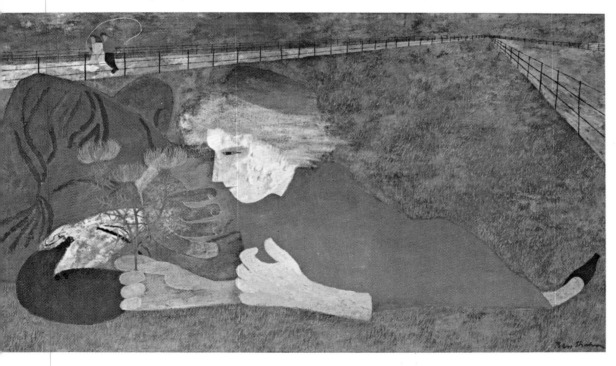

SUN AND ROCKS by Charles E. Burchfield (1893-   ). Albright-Knox Art Gallery,
Room of Contemporary Art Fund, Buffalo, New York.

"Stand aside
And clear out of my path;
I will not be denied,"

The swaggering sun in his wrath
Cried out of the cloud.

MELVILLE CANE (1879-   )
From "Sun and Cloud"

128

SUNRISE by Arthur G. Dove (1880-1946). Oil. Courtesy of Milwaukee Art Center.

Young palmer sun, that to these shining sands
  Pourest thy pilgrim's tale, discoursing still
Thy silver passages of sacred lands,
  With news of Sepulchre and Dolorous Hill. . . .

SIDNEY LANIER (1842-1881)
From "A Sunrise Song"

Oh for the face and footstep! — Woods and shores
That looked upon us in life's happiest flush,
That saw our figures breaking from the brush;
That heard our voices calling through the bowers. . . .

FREDERICK GODDARD TUCKERMAN (1821-1873)
From *The Sonnets of Frederick Goddard Tuckerman*

TWO GIRLS FISHING by John Singer Sargent (1856-1925).
From the permanent collections of the Cincinnati Art Museum.

A DAY IN JUNE by George Wesley Bellows (1882-1925).
Collection of The Detroit Institute of Arts.

The day is fresh-washed and fair,

and there is a smell of tulips and narcissus in the air.

AMY LOWELL (1874-1925)
From "Spring Day"

So detached and cool she is
No motion e'er betrays
The secret life within her soul,
The anguish of her days.

CLARISSA SCOTT DELANY (1901-1926)
From "The Mask"

AFTERNOON by Andrew Wyeth (1917-   ).
Egg tempera on panel. Courtesy Milwaukee Art Center.

OVERLEAF

QUAKER LADIES by Andrew Wyeth (1917-   ). Dry brush.
Collection of Mr. and Mrs. H. F. du Pont, Wilmington, Delaware.

My eyes in the sun-swimming clouds,
I soar toward heights I can never reach,
Nor see that I am crushing loveliness
Beneath my wingless feet.

GLORIA GODDARD (1889-   )
From "To the Commonplace"

CORN by John Steuart Curry (1897-1946). Wichita Art Museum,
Roland P. Murdock Collection, Wichita, Kansas.

ROASTING EARS by Thomas Hart Benton (1889-   ). Tempera with oil glazes. The Metropolitan Museum of Art, Arthur H. Hearn Fund.

Tall timber stood here once, here on a corn belt farm
       along the Monon.
Here the roots of a half mile of tree dug their
       runners deep in the loam for a grip and a hold
       against wind storms.

CARL SANDBURG (1878-   )
From "Improved Farm Land"

The wind blows. The corn leans. The corn leaves go rustling. The march time and the windbeat is on October drums. The stalks of fodder bend all the way, the way the last windstorm passed.

CARL SANDBURG (1878-   )
From "Ripe Corn"

135

CORN by John Rogers Cox (1915-   ). Mr. and Mrs. Benjamin G. Cox.

But now again my mind turns to the glorious corn. See it — look on its ripening, waving field. See how it wears a crown, prouder than monarch ever was; sometimes jauntily and sometimes after the storm, the dignified survivors of the tempest seem to view a field of slaughter and to pity a fallen foe.

RICHARD J. OGLESBY (1824-1899)
From an Address

WHITE CLOUD by John Rogers Cox (1915-   ). Courtesy of Dr. Howard Laufman.

Desirous cloud, we are too wan

For day or night to build upon,

And all our dream of happiness

Goes up in steam, comes down in less.

SAMUEL HOFFENSTEIN (1890-1947)
From "Cloud"

OVERLEAF

THE SCARECROW by Andrew Wyeth (1917-   ). Mixed media.
ART:USA, The Johnson Collection of Contemporary American Paintings.

Facing a cold and sneering sky,

   Cold as the sneering hearts of men,

A man began to prophesy,

   To speak of love and faith again.

LOUIS UNTERMEYER (1885-   )
From "Two Funerals"

THE HUNT by William Gropper (1897-   ).
The Metropolitan Museum of Art, George A. Hearn Fund, 1937.

140

The way ran under boughs of checkered green
Where live things stirred, and sweet lights glinted through,
And airs were cooled and scented. . . .

RICHARD BURTON (1861-1940)
From "Wood Witchery"

THE WATERFALL by John H. Twachtman (1853-1902). Oil.
The Metropolitan Museum of Art, gift of George A. Hearn, 1909.

The noise of water teased his literal ears

Which heard the distant drumming and thus scored:

Water is falling — it fell — therefore it roared.

But he cried, That is more than water I hear.

JOHN CROWE RANSOM (1888-   )
From "Persistent Explorer"

. . . All day long [the rescue boat] had poked up and down cypress- and gum-choked bayous and across cotton fields (where at times instead of swimming it waded) gathering its sorry cargo from the tops of houses and barns and even out of trees, and now it warped into that mushroom city of the forlorn and despairing where kerosene flares smoked in the drizzle and hurriedly strung electrics glared upon the bayonets of martial policemen and the red cross brassards of doctors and nurses and canteen-workers.

WILLIAM FAULKNER (1897-1962)
From *The Old Man*

THE MISSISSIPPI by John Steuart Curry (1897-1946).
Collection City Art Museum of Saint Louis.

These lovely graves of fountain-trees that shake
    A burning spray against autumnal cool,
Descend again in molten drops to make
    The rutted path a river and a pool.

They rise in silence, fall in quietude,
    Lie still as looking-glass in every sense;
Only their lion-color in the wood
    Roars to miraculous heat and turbulence.

ELINOR WYLIE (1885-1928)
"Golden Bough"

GOLDEN AUTUMN by William Thon (1906-   ). Courtesy Midtown Galleries.

144

AUTUMN FIELD by Mark Tobey (1890-   ). Tempera.
ART:USA, The Johnson Collection of Contemporary American Paintings.

a wind has blown the rain away and blown

the sky away and all the leaves away,

and the trees stand. I think i too have known

autumn too long. . . .

E. E. CUMMINGS (1894-1962)
From "a wind has blown the rain away and blown"

IN THE CONNECTICUT HILLS by Ben Foster (1852-1926).
Metropolitan Museum of Art, N.Y.

Earth, my likeness,

Though you look so impassive, ample and spheric there,

I now suspect that is not all;

I now suspect there is something fierce in you eligible to

    burst forth....

WALT WHITMAN (1819-1892)
From "Earth, My Likeness"

Who knows to-day from yesterday
May learn to count no thing too strange:
Love builds of what Time takes away,
Till Death itself is less than Change.

EDWARD ARLINGTON ROBINSON (1869-1935)
From "Hillcrest"

ABOVE THE EARTH by Mark Tobey (1890-   ). Gouache on cardboard.
Courtesy of The Art Institute of Chicago, gift of Mr. and Mrs. Sigmund Kunstadter.

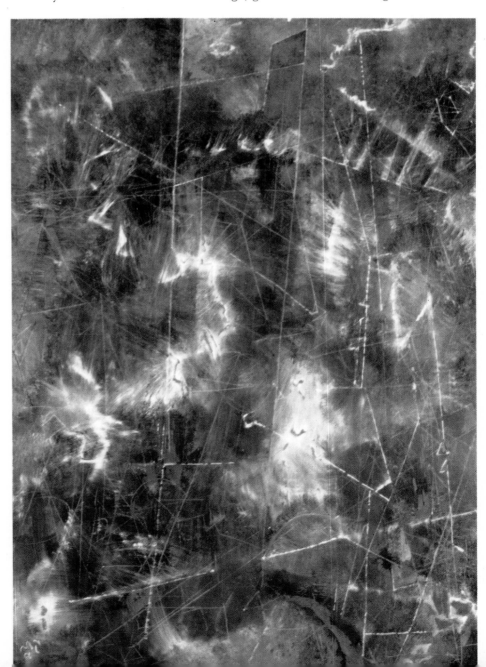

There will, indeed, be modification of landscape,

And in margin of natural disaster, substantial reduction.

There will be refinement of principle, and purified action,

And expansion, we trust, of human heart-hope, and hand-scope.

ROBERT PENN WARREN (1905-   )
From "Infant Boy at Midcentury: Modification of Landscape"

THE ARTIST LOOKS AT NATURE by Charles Sheeler (1883-1965). Oil.
Courtesy of The Art Institute of Chicago, gift of the Society for Contemporary American Art.

Camera Clix, Inc.

Smile O voluptuous cool-breath'd earth!

Earth of the slumbering and liquid trees!

Earth of departed sunset — earth of the mountains
*   mistytopt!*

Earth of the vitreous pour of the full moon just tinged
*   with blue!*

Earth of shine and dark mottling the tide of the river!

Earth of the limpid gray of clouds brighter and clearer
*   for my sake!*

WALT WHITMAN (1819-1892)
From "Song of Myself"

THE NORTH COUNTRY by Willard L. Metcalf (1858-1925).
The Metropolitan Museum of Art, George A. Hearn Fund, 1924.

151

LIGHTS OF OTHER DAYS by John Frederick Peto (1854-1907).
Oil. Courtesy of The Art Institute of Chicago, Goodman Fund.

VI
The Interior Life

All truths wait in all things,

They neither hasten their own delivery nor resist it,

They do not need the obstetric forceps of the surgeon,

The insignificant is as big to me as any....

WALT WHITMAN (1819-1892)
From "Song of Myself"

I heard . . . oh voiceless trees
Under the wind, I knew
The eager terrible spring
Hidden in you.

SARA TEASDALE (1884-1933)
From "February"

LILLIES by Peter Blume (1906-   ).
Museum of Fine Arts, Boston.

154

The bustle in a house
  The morning after death
Is solemnest of industries
  Enacted upon earth —

The sweeping up the heart,
  And putting love away
We shall not want to use again
  Until eternity.

EMILY DICKINSON (1830-1886)
"The bustle in a house"

JUST DESSERT by William Michael Harnett (1848-1892). Oil.
Courtesy of The Art Institute of Chicago, Friends of American Art Collection.

156

MARKET BASKET, HAT AND UMBRELLA by John Frederick Peto (1854-1907).
Courtesy of Milwaukee Art Center.

Here rest, their keen vibrations mute,

The shout of voices known so well,

The ringing laugh, the wailing flute,

The chiding of the sharp-tongued bell.

OLIVER WENDELL HOLMES (1809-1894)
From "Mare Rubrum"

157

Music I heard with you was more
than music,
And bread I broke with you was
more than bread;
Now that I am without you, all
is desolate;
All that was once so beautiful
is dead.

CONRAD AIKEN (1889-   )
From "Music I Heard with You"

THAT WHICH I SHOULD HAVE DONE
I DID NOT DO by Ivan Albright (1897-   ).
Oil. Courtesy of The Art Institute of Chicago.

FRUIT ON A PEWTER PLATE by Rubens Peale (1784-1865).
Courtesy of Milwaukee Art Center.

December is howling,
But feign it a flute:
Help on the deceiving —
Paint flowers and fruit!

HERMAN MELVILLE (1819-1891)
From "Fruit and Flower Painter"

OVERLEAF

FRUIT AND FLOWERS by unknown American primitive artist about 1835.
From the Collection of Edgar William and Bernice Chrysler Garbisch.

INDEX OF ARTISTS

INDEX OF AUTHORS